NAPA VALLEY
The Delaplaine
2021 Long Weekend Guide

Andrew Delaplaine

NO BUSINESS HAS PAID A SINGLE PENNY OR GIVEN _ANYTHING_ TO BE INCLUDED IN THIS BOOK.

GET 3 FREE NOVELS
Like political thrillers?
See next page to download 3 great page-turners—
FREE - no strings attached.

Senior Editors - *Renee & Sophie Delaplaine*
Senior Writer - **James Cubby**

Gramercy Park Press
New York London Paris

WANT 3 **FREE** THRILLERS?

Why, of course you do!

If you like these writers--

Vince Flynn, Brad Thor, Tom Clancy, James Patterson, David Baldacci, John Grisham, Brad Meltzer, Daniel Silva, Don DeLillo

If you like these TV series –

House of Cards, Scandal, West Wing, The Good Wife, Madam Secretary, Designated Survivor

---

You'll love the **unputdownable** series about Jack Houston St. Clair, with political intrigue, romance, and loads of action and suspense.

Besides writing travel books, I've written political thrillers for many years that have delighted hundreds of thousands of readers. I want to introduce you to my work!
Send me an email and I'll send you a link where you can download the first 3 books in my bestselling series, absolutely FREE.

Mention **this book** when you email me.
andrewdelaplaine@mac.com

2

NAPA VALLEY
The Delaplaine
Long Weekend Guide

TABLES OF CONTENTS

WHY NAPA VALLEY?

Depending on the time of year, there's nothing more fun than taking a trip out to the wine country, especially Napa and Sonoma counties. In fact, after you make your first trip, you'll come back and focus on this special part of America, so completely a world unto itself that there's literally nothing else like it in this country. I am in the wine trade myself (my family produces a fine sparkling wine using grapes from Napa and Sonoma), so I know a little bit about it.

The two valleys are just an hour's drive north of San Francisco.

The two counties are quite different in layout and attitude. Though Napa is more famous than Sonoma, winemaking actually began in Sonoma (in 1835) a whole generation before vineyards were planted in the 35-mile long Napa Valley. And while vineyards line Napa from one end to the other, in

Sonoma there still are fields where vineyards have not been planted.

While Napa is narrow and more confined, in Sonoma, the land extends out from the Russian River far and wide, giving you a much more expansive sensation. Between Napa and Sonoma, there are hundreds of wineries large and small. Napa has some 45,000 acres planted with grapes. While Napa has all the celebrities, the high-end restaurants, the luxurious spas, Sonoma really feels like a rustic farming area by comparison. Much less razzmatazz. The good thing about both valleys is that they're right next to each other, so it's easy to enjoy both. But here our focus is on Napa.

Wine lovers didn't really begin flocking to this area until the 1980s, and the lodgings at the time were limited to a few inns and some B&Bs.

These days, however, you'll find superior lodgings to match anywhere in the world, complementing the high quality of the wines produced here.

Nobody thinks of this, but did you know there's a **Veterans Home** in Yountville? Now, I ask you, if you had been in the military, wouldn't you want to retire here?

GETTING ABOUT

Most people come to Napa by way of San Francisco, and the town of Napa itself is only 55 miles from San Francisco. The towns strung along the Valley moving north are: Napa, Yountville, Oakville, Rutherford, St. Helena and Calistoga. Sonoma County is just a few miles to the east of Napa Valley.

The Valley is only 35 miles from one end to the other, so (traffic permitting) it only takes a half hour to go from Napa in the south to Calistoga in the north on Hwy. 29 (also known as the St. Helena Hwy.).

The **Silverado Trail**, some 2 miles away, run parallel to Hwy. 29, and during peak traffic, makes a faster alternative if you're in a hurry. Also has splendid views.

High season runs from March through the harvest in October, and this is when the place is jammed with tourists. I heartily advise people making their second trip to come in those fringe areas of the off-season, early March or early November, let's say, to get a sense of what it's like to really live here. Deals are more easily had in the off-season, of course, and you end up spending more time with the locals than you (or they) have time for in the crush of summer.

The drunk driving laws are very severe in California, and they are firmly enforced. Even if you drive up, unless you have a dedicated driver, it sometimes is a good idea to hire a driver. These drivers also act as tour guides, so you're getting a lot more than the ride.

BUS SERVICE
There is a bus service called **The Vine** running up and down the Valley that's easy to use.
http://www.ridethevine.com/

HIRE A DRIVER

ST. HELENA WINE TOURS
1541 Chablis Cir, St Helena, 707-963-9644
Fleet has Jaguar sedans, vans for larger parties, stretch limos and Lincoln Navigators. Rates from $60/hour. (Ken Slavens is often recommended if you want to ask for someone specific.) Wide range of

wine tours. They'll also do "dinner runs" if you want
a taxi service. Check for rates.

PERATA LUXURY TOURS
707-227-8271
www.perataluxurycarservices.com/
Personalized wine tours, dinner trips, airport service,
and just about anything else you want. From $68 per
hour, with minimum hourly requirements. They use
Chevy Suburbans.

VISITOR INFORMATION

Napa Valley Conference & Visitors Center
1310 Napa Town Center, Napa: 707-226-7459
www.napavalley.com
Comprehensive information on lodgings, restaurants,
spas, activities while you're there, wineries. (They
have a winery map you can just print out a copy on
their web site).

WHERE TO STAY

DID YOU FIND AN INTERESTING PLACE?
If you discover a place you think I should check out
on my next visit, drop me a line, will you? I'll
mention your name if I end up listing it.
andrewdelaplaine@mac.com

ARBOR GUEST HOUSE
1436 G St., Napa: 707-252-8144 SEP
arborguesthouse.com
This B&B has 3 suites in the main house and 2 suites
in the Carriage House. This timeless estate features an
enchanting gazebo and tranquil sitting areas
throughout the garden where guests can relax their
minds and forget the rush of everyday life, play a

mellow game of bocce ball or stroll the beautifully cultivated grounds. Retire to the living room for afternoon wine with nosh or relax and read the paper by the fire.

ANDAZ NAPA
1450 First St., Napa: 707-687-1234
www.napa.andaz.hyatt.com
Right in downtown Napa, the Andaz makes an excellent choice if you want to explore the 14 tasting rooms in the immediate area featuring some of the best wines in California. All the usual amenities. (A Hyatt property.)

AUBERGE DU SOLEIL RESORT
180 Rutherford Hill Rd., Rutherford: 800-348-5406
aubergedusoleil.com
Since 1985, this has been a top place to stay. They have a collection of sun- and earth-toned rooms and suites, each featuring French doors opening onto private terraces, cozy fireplaces and sensuous elements such as private soaking tubs for two. For the Auberge's signature style of soft-spoken luxury, the partners tapped renowned designer Michael Taylor,

who infused his dramatic California style with the essence of Provence. Full spa services. (Try the milk chocolate bath in-suite, for a touch of decadence.) Certainly one of Napa's most luxurious resorts, with one of the area's best restaurants, the **Bistro & Bar**. Since it's really pricey, check out the Bistro first. Here you can order a couple of small plates to taste and get a glass of wine, and not break the budget while taking advantage of the sunset on the terrace or the fire crackling inside.

BARDESSONO
6526 Yount St., Yountville: 707-204-6000
www.bardessono.com/spa/
They have 62 rooms in downtown Yountville. Each is designed for in-room spa services. The menu in the restaurant here is based on local, farm-fresh ingredients. A real treat is the rooftop pool where you can also dine. I've been all over the world, but I've never seen a menu item reading "freshly dug carrot salad." I'm tempted to write that it's "so freshly dug you can still taste the dirt on the carrot," but I'm not. (In any case, go for the parsnip soup—it's really good.) They have a wide selection of fish here, and it's painstakingly prepared, but don't overlook the

lamb T-bone: you almost never see that cut (it's served with fennel, squash and "saffron spaetzle," and it's excellent).

BEAZLEY HOUSE
1910 First St., Napa: 707-257-1649
beazleyhouse.com
"Napa's first & still its finest bed & breakfast nn." Or so they say. It really is a nice place, a beautifully converted old house. Jim and Carol Beazley set up shop in 1981. You stay in rooms in either the Mansion or the Carriage House (opened in 1983), which has 5 rooms, each with its own entrance, fireplace, 2-person tub. The Beazley House is just a short walk from the newly revitalized downtown Napa riverfront, the Opera House, the Wine Train, fine dining, shopping, and Napa's Oxbow Market.

Dog friendly, free Internet access, tasty breakfasts made in-house, lovely gardens. And they're always sprucing up the place.

CALISTOGA RANCH
580 Lommel Rd., Calistoga: 855-942-4220
www.calistogaranch.com/
The "lodges" here offer private patios, fireplaces, great views of the 150+ acre compound. Oak groves abound, so you're really quite in the country. Very posh. Yoga deck. Expensive, of course, starting from $900. Very private, facilities and grounds top-notch. (Take a look into their wine cave. Kind of eerie.)

CANDLELIGHT INN
1045 Easum Dr., Napa: 707-257-3717
candlelightinn.com
Candlelight Inn — a luxurious Napa Valley B&B. Located near downtown Napa, this lovely 1929 English Tudor inn is centrally located to all the wonders of wine country, yet oh, so far away. Situated on an acre of land beneath towering redwood trees along the banks of the Napa Creek, this place feels like a park. A romantic and restful backyard, manicured gardens and a gorgeous swimming pool.

CARNEROS INN
4048 Sonoma Hwy., Napa: 707-299-4900
https://carnerosresort.com
You can see for miles from the vantage point of the rise where the inn is situated. There are almost no trees obstructing the view, which gives the place a rather Spartan feel, but it's quite luxurious. Great

lodgings, restaurant and bar. Open and airy, lots of windows.

CEDAR GABLES INN
486 Coombs St., Napa: 707-224-7969
cedargablesinn.com
A luxurious 10,000 square foot mansion made into a B&B. They offer a 3-course gourmet breakfast, evening hors d'oeuvres and wine tasting. It's all quite grand for a B&B, but you won't argue.
Napa Cooking Classes
Paired with outstanding wines from the best wine producing region in the world, the Cedar Gables Inn Cooking School offers the ultimate Napa Culinary Experience: Hands on cooking classes with top notch chefs from the area. Following the class you get to eat what you made in the Inn's elegant dining room.

CHELSEA GARDEN INN
1443 Second St., Calistoga: 707-942-0948

chelseagardeninn.com

Set among lush garden paths, Chelsea Garden Inn has one-bedroom suites with private entrances, private baths and fireplaces. Has a seasonal pool, jasmine-lined walkways, whimsical touches, bold colors, fine linens, down pillows, and other amenities in every private suite.

GOLDEN HAVEN HOT SPRINGS SPA AND RESORT

1713 Lake St., Calistoga: 707-942-8000
goldenhaven.com

Calistoga hot springs water and rejuvenating spa treatments. After a day of touring Napa Valley, you can swim in their hot springs pool, relax on the sun deck, plop into a mud bath and otherwise perk up with their Calistoga spa treatments.

HARVEST INN

1 Main St, St Helena, 707-963-9463
www.harvestinn.com/

Set on 8 acres of vineyards, this upscale resort inn offers 74 guest rooms and suites – each unique and charming, many with fireplaces. Amenities include:

free Wi-Fi, flat-screen TVs, and free breakfast. Hotel facilities include: private decks, 2 heated outdoor pools, 2 hot tubs, exercise room, fireside wine bar with a grand piano, and spa treatments (fee).

HENNESSEY HOUSE
1727 Main St., Napa: 707-226-3774
hennesseyhouse.com
Downtown Napa just a stroll away from this wonderful Queen Anne style house built in the 1890s. (The porch was added in 1901.) Eggs Florentine for breakfast. Fireplaces, two-person whirlpool tubs and featherbeds in some rooms. The place is stuffed with great antiques. Very comfy.

HOTEL YOUNTVILLE
6462 Washington St., Yountville: 707-967-7900
www.hotelyountville.com/
You don't even need a car when you get here. So many great places to eat are within walking distance, you could spend a week here and never get in a car.

Lots of little boutiques for shopping, and 4 wine tasting rooms nearby. Their concierge will help you navigate the Napa area if you want them to. Free bikes. Let them know what you're interested in before you arrive and they'll map out what you need to do to see it all. **Spa AcQua** is located here. They have 6 treatment rooms, 2 couple's "spa suites" featuring Vichy showers, luxurious double hydrotherapy tubs and fireplaces. Decadent? Oh, yes. Check out their web site to see the kind of specially priced packages they offer that might apply to you when you travel. (Especially good off-season.)

INDIAN SPRINGS
1712 Lincoln Ave., Calistoga: 707-709-8139
indianspringscalistoga.com
Lovely palm tree-lined drive takes you to this historic spa resort at the northern end of the Napa Valley. California's oldest continuously operating pool and spa facility. Situated on 16 acres planted with olive and palm trees, roses and lavender, the property has 4 thermal geysers that produce an extraordinary supply of rich mineral water. Another prized asset is the vast, natural deposit of pure volcanic ash on the acreage.

INN ON RANDOLPH
411 Randolph St., Napa: 707-257-2886
innonrandolph.com
Located in heart of downtown Napa, it's only a short walk to over a dozen tasting rooms, popular restaurants, evening activities and local events.

LAS ALCOBAS
1915 Main St, St. Helena, 707-963-7000
www.starwoodhotels.com
Overlooking the Spring Mountains, this luxurious vineyard resort hotel offers a nice selection of guest rooms and suites, many of which overlook a working vineyard with views of forests rising over the rolling hills in the distance. Though the building is old, the décor is ultra-modern, very sleek. Wonderfully, some rooms have bathtubs that are outside on private balconies overlooking the vineyard. Definitely try to get a corner room so you have two views. The expansive floor-to-ceiling windows make the most of these incredible views. Amenities: Complimentary breakfast and Wi-Fi, flat-screen TVs and lots of quality "freebies." Hotel features: an airy spa, a yoga studio, a gym, on-site restaurant, heated outdoor pool with cabanas and a pool bar. Conveniently located just 2 miles from the 19th-century Freemark Abbey Winery and a 13-minute walk from the historic St. Helena Catholic Church.

LAVENDER
2020 Webber Ave., Yountville: 707-944-1388
lavendernapa.com
What they've achieved here is a combination of modern luxuries and top-notch services and given it all the look and feel of a B&B. "Conde Nast Traveler" voted it one the "Top 50 Small Hotels," and that's no accident. An old house forms the center of complex of 4 buildings. There's a wraparound porch, an enclosed verandah where breakfast is served.

They've made every effort to give you the feeling you're in Provence. (And they come damn close.)

MAISON FLEURIE
6529 Yount St., Yountville: 707-944-2056
www.maisonfleurienapa.com
Charming (and not too costly) B&B in ivy-covered stone buildings dating back to the 1870s. Better than average breakfast. Wine and canapés in the late afternoon. Lovely gardens.

MEADOWOOD
900 Meadowood Lane, St. Helena: 707-531-4788
www.meadowood.com
Luxurious resort in a splendid country setting. They do everything here: weddings, sporting events (they have a pool, tennis courts, golf), conferences, events and a wide variety of seasonal offerings (like a Thanksgiving special that's very nice). It's one thing

to see how "the other half" live, but here you can see how they relax.

From $650 to over $1,000 per night. (If you're a foodie, you'll want to know that **The Restaurant at Meadowood** has 3 stars from Michelin, but if you're foodie .)

MILLIKEN CREEK INN & SPA
1815 Silverado Trail, Napa, 707-255-1197
www.millikencreekinn.com
Set on 3 acres overlooking the Napa River, this beautiful inn & spa offers 12 elegant rooms. Amenities include: free Wi-Fi, flat-screen TVs, minibars, whirlpool tubs, and free breakfast (in your room if you like—get the homemade granola with sunflower seeds) and evening wine reception. Hotel features include: Oversized hydrotherapy tubs with green tea bath salts and on-site spa offering holistic and therapeutic treatments, massages and facials.

THE NAPA INN
1137 Warren St., Napa: 707-257-1444
napainn.com
14 rooms and suites are individually decorated. Each has private bathroom and fireplace. Some have two-person whirlpool tubs and all have showers. The Napa Inn observes Eco-friendly practices. A gourmet candlelight breakfast is served each morning in the Napa Inn dining room or on the garden patio. Evening wine and refreshments.

NORTH BLOCK HOTEL
6757 Washington St, Yountville, 707-944-8080

www.northblockhotel.com
Mediterranean-inspired hotel offering elegant rooms
with private balconies or patios. Amenities include:
free Wi-Fi, flat-screen TVs, soaking tubs and
espresso machines. Hotel facilities include: heated
outdoor pool, fitness center and spa (fee). On-site
upscale Italian restaurant.

OLD WORLD INN
1301 Jefferson St., Napa: 707-257-0112
oldworldinn.com
As one of Napa's first bed and breakfasts, the Old
World Inn is known for two things: home-style food
and friendliness. You get freshly baked chocolate
chip cookies when you check in. At 5:30, hey have a
little wine reception. You get chocolate desserts when
you return to the Inn each evening. Two-course
breakfast is served.

PETIT LOGIS
6527 Yount St., Yountville: 877-944-2332
www.petitlogis.com/
Completely seductive inn with only 5 rooms. It's not
a B&B in the sense that there's no breakfast. (But
there's the famous **Bouchon Bakery** just next door
where you can get a REALLY great morning snack!
They open at 7 a.m., by the way.) The rooms here,
while comfy and rustic (they even have fireplaces),
still offer completely updated amenities: big
bathrooms, Jacuzzi tubs, refrigerators, wireless
Internet. Great restaurants like the **French Laundry**
are just down the street.

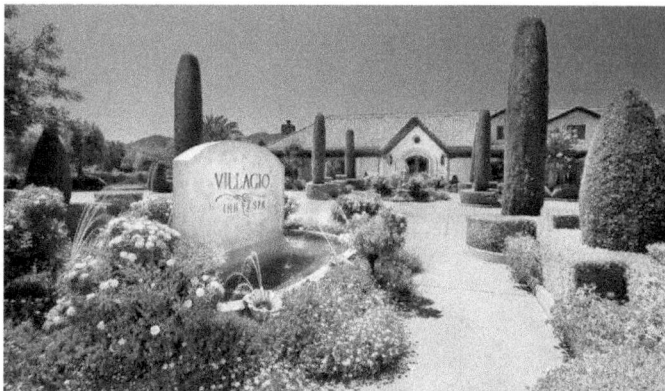

VILLAGIO INN & SPA
6481 Washington St., Yountville: 707-927-2130
villagio.com
Located on the 23-acre Vintage Estate, Villagio Inn &
Spa has been dubbed by "Town & Country"
Magazine as a "pleasure seeker's heaven." This
Tuscan-inspired Yountville hotel property features
flowing water fountain pathways weaved throughout
lush Mediterranean-style gardens. The San Francisco
Chronicle Magazine described their rooms and suites
as "massive, terribly tasteful and terribly elegant."
You'll agree. This is a much larger place than most
lodgings you find in the area. Free bottle of white
wine when you arrive. Charming, with balconies,
porches, fireplaces, Jacuzzi in your room.

WHERE TO EAT

Napa
Yountville
Rutherford
St. Helena
Calitoga

DID YOU FIND AN INTERESTING PLACE?
If you discover a place you think I should check out
on my next visit, drop me a line, will you? I'll
mention your name if I end up listing it.
andrewdelaplaine@mac.com

NAPA

ALEXIS BAKING COMPANY AND CAFÉ
1517 3rd St, Napa, 707-258-1827
www.abcnapa.com

CUISINE: Breakfast/Bakery
DRINKS: No Booze
SERVING: Breakfast & Lunch
PRICE RANGE: $$
Popular bakery & cafe offering creative breakfast menu, daily lunch specials and a selection of homemade bread and pastries. Menu picks include: Lemon ricotta pancakes and huevos rancheros.

ANGELE
540 Main St., Napa: 707-252-8115
angelerestaurant.com
CUISINE: French
DRINKS: Full Bar
SERVING: Lunch / Dinner
Has a menu that layers elements from traditional recipes with contemporary influences. Its focus on rich and soothing French cuisine ranges from the classic simplicity of fresh, seasonal salads to the robust balance of bœuf bourguignon. Whether seated at a table in the dining room, at the full bar or outside on the terrace overlooking the Napa River, enjoy

lunch and dinner surrounded by a simple, family-style setting.

AZZURRO PIZZERIA E ENOTECA
1260 Main St, Napa, 707-255-5552
www.azzurropizzeria.com
CUISINE: Pizza / Italian
DRINKS: Beer & Wine Only
SERVING: Lunch & Dinner
PRICE RANGE: $$
Busy Italian pizzeria serving thin-crust pizzas that come from a wood-fired oven (arguably the best in town), small plates, pastas, sandwiches, and antipasti. Italian eatery known for thin-crust pizzas plus small plates, pastas & lots of local wines. Favorites include: Wedge Salad (loaded with bacon bits, nuts, and other vegetables) and the Speck pizza made with slices of cured meat and fresh mozzarella.

BISTRO DON GIOVANNI
4110 Howard Ln., Napa: 707-224-3300
bistrodongiovanni.com
CUISINE: Italian
DRINKS: Full Bar
SERVING: Lunch/ Dinner
The best tasting meals are prepared simply, and with the freshest ingredients. They source their herbs, vegetables and produce from local farmers and support ranches that raise humanely-treated, free-roaming livestock and poultry. All of the menu items are inspired by the bounty of the region and prepared with utmost attention to detail. Donna's way of selecting and combining seasonal products to highlight pure, robust flavors in an ever changing variety has drawn a steady stream of loyal diners. Great wine list, of course.

CA' MOMI OSTERIA
1141 1st St, Napa, 707-224-6664
www.camomiosteria.com
CUISINE: Pizza / Italian
DRINKS: Full Bar
SERVING: Breakfast, Lunch & Dinner
PRICE RANGE: $$
Known for their authentic Neapolitan style pizzas,
they also serve a variety of other Italian dishes.
Indoor and outdoor seating. On-site wine shop.

CELADON
500 Main St., Napa: 707-254-9690
celadonnapa.com
CUISINE: International; seafood
DRINKS: Full Bar
SERVING: Lunch/ Dinner
Enjoy Celadon's award-winning 'Global Comfort
Food' in their beautiful dining room or out in the
lovely courtyard. The seasonally influenced menu
features flavors from the Mediterranean, Asia, and the
Americas.

GOTT'S ROADSIDE
644 1st St, Napa, 707-224-6900
www.gotts.com
CUISINE: American (New) / Burgers
DRINKS: Beer & Wine Only
SERVING: Breakfast, Lunch & Dinner
PRICE RANGE: $$
A self-serve joint with picnic tables offering a menu
of creative burgers like the Western Bacon Blue Ring
Burger. The burgers are great but the also make a
delicious Ahi tuna burger, salads, and tacos. One of
their thick chocolate shakes is the perfect pairing for
one of their fat burgers.

HERITAGE EATS
3824 Bel Aire Plaza, Napa, 707-226-3287
www.heritageeats.com
CUISINE: Mexican
DRINKS: Full Bar
SERVING: Lunch & Dinner

PRICE RANGE: $$
NEIGHBORHOOD: Downtown
Located in Whole Foods Plaza, this fast-casual eatery offers a selection of cuisines from Vietnam, Thailand, Jamaica and Mexico served cafeteria-style. Wide selection of local and global beers, wines (with a really good selection of half-bottles—perfect for lunch) and healthy non-alcoholic beverages. Favorites: Jamaican Jerk Chicken baos and Lemongrass pork baos.

HOG ISLAND OYSTER COMPANY
610 1st St #22, Napa, 707-251-8113
www.hogislandoysters.com
CUISINE: Seafood
DRINKS: Beer & Wine Only

SERVING: Lunch & Dinner
PRICE RANGE: $$

Foodies love this modern oyster bar that offers a creative menu of seafood and organic fare. Menu picks: Oysters (of course) and Halibut.

THE KITCHEN DOOR
610 1st St #24, Napa, 707-226-1560
www.kitchendoornapa.com
CUISINE: American (New) / Pizza
DRINKS: Beer & Wine Only
SERVING: Lunch & Dinner
PRICE RANGE: $$
Casual market café offering an ingredient-driven menu. Menu picks: Chicken wings and Mushroom pizza. Located inside the Oxbrow Market so you can shop and eat. Outdoor seating available.

LA TABERNA
815 Main St, Napa, 707-224-5551
www.latabernanapa.com
CUISINE: Spanish/Tapas/Small plates
DRINKS: Full Bar
SERVING: Dinner; closed Mondays
PRICE RANGE: $$
Contemporary eatery offering a menu of Spanish tapas/small plates in the *pintxos* style. That means it's a tapas bar but with a Basque slant like you find in San Sebastian. Very innovative for these parts. A huge selection of Spanish wines is on hand, which is a refreshing change from the California-heavy lists you normally encounter in this area. While the menu changes quite frequently, they usually have suckling pig, which is fabulous. Other favorites: Lamb empanadas and Tuna bocadillo.

LA TOQUE

1314 McKinstry St., Napa: 707-257-5157
latoque.com
CUISINE: American; French
DRINKS: Full Bar
SERVING: Dinner

The menu evolves constantly to show off each season's finest ingredients. They have developed a network of local farmers and purveyors who supply them with some of the finest foods in the world. The Options menu is presented in three sections from which you can create your own multi-course experience. Their Chef's Tasting Menu and Vegetable Tasting Menu are presented in a fixed format of five courses.

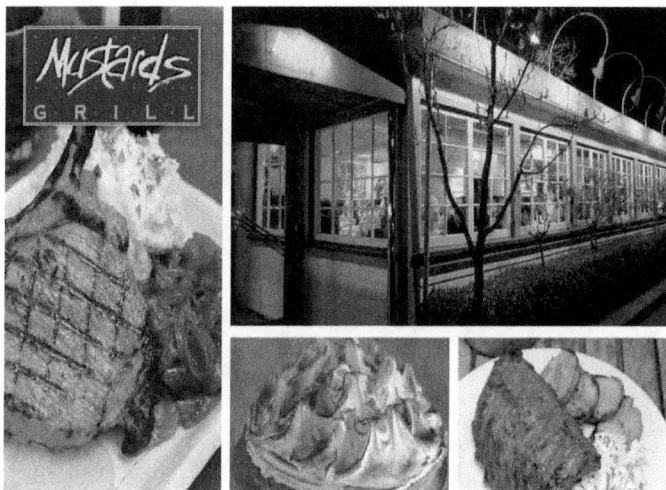

MUSTARDS GRILL
7399 Saint Helena Hwy., Napa: 707-944-2424
www.mustardsgrill.com/
CUISINE: American
DRINKS: Full bar
SERVING: Lunch, Dinner
No class distinctions here. You'll find local cops and firefighters plopping down for this excellent food, sitting right next to famous celebrities, including Bobby Flay, who said the Mongolian pork chop he ate here was one of the best dishes he ever ate.

NORMAN ROSE TAVERN
1401 1st St, Napa, 707-258-1516
www.normanrosenapa.com
CUISINE: American (New) / Exalted Pub fare
DRINKS: Full Bar
SERVING: Lunch & Dinner
PRICE RANGE: $$

Neighborhood pub with a menu of classic pub fare using locally sourced ingredients. Menu picks include: grilled pork chops; buttermilk fried chicken sandwich; Grilled chicken salad with candied pecans & pears and the All American Grilled cheese.

OENOTRI
1425 First St., Napa: 707-252-1022
oenotri.com
CUISINE: Italian
DRINKS: Full Bar
SERVING: Lunch/ Dinner

Oenotri is an Italian restaurant in downtown Napa featuring a daily changing menu driven by ingredients that are local, fresh and in season. They celebrate culinary traditions rarely seen elsewhere in California — the specialties of Sicily, Campania, Calabria, Basilicata and Puglia. Salumi is handcrafted in house, and their pasta is made fresh daily, and ALL their pasta selection are standouts. As part of their goal to serve quality artisanal pizza, they imported a wood-fueled Acino oven from Naples to bake authentic pizza Napoletana.

RESTAURANT AT CIA AT COPIA
500 1st St, Napa, 707-967-2500
www.ciaatcopia.com
CUISINE: American (New)
DRINKS: Full Bar
SERVING: Lunch & Dinner
PRICE RANGE: $$
The **Culinary Institute of America** (CIA), the CIA at Copia, is the ultimate Napa Valley destination offering food, wine, cooking and beverage classes, wine tastings, a lifestyle store, art collections, and a full-service bar and restaurant. The elegantly decorated restaurant is casual, but the food is top-notch. Favorites: Braised beef tongue and Seared halibut. Gluten-free options.

TORC
1140 Main St, Napa, 707-252-3292
www.torcnapa.com
CUISINE: American (New)
DRINKS: Full Bar

SERVING: Dinner; closed Tuesday
PRICE RANGE: $$$
Beautiful rustic eatery with a farm-to-table menu.
Favorites: Soft shell crab taco, roasted chicken for 2
(really tasty, and what comes with it changes based
on what they got that morning from the farmers'
market) and a damned fine Tomato Tart that's
heavenly. Open kitchen, creative cocktails and
impressive wine list loaded up with Napa specialties.
Daily happy hour with tasty happy hour menu.

VINTNER'S COLLECTIVE TASTING ROOM
1245 Main St., Napa: 707-255-7150
www.**vintnerscollective**.com
Another great spot for tasting the wines of many
different wineries, all under the roof of an historic
building that has been restored. The building has an
interesting history all its own: it formerly housed a
brothel, a brewery, a laundry, a meat company and a
saloon.

ZUZU
829 Main St., Napa: 707-224-8555

http://www.zuzunapa.com/
CUISINE: Spanish Tapas
DRINKS: Beer/ Wine
SERVING: Lunch/ Dinner/ Weekends dinner only
The restaurant offers a modern, California version of
tapas along with some traditional offerings based on
the cuisines of Spain, Portugal and the Mediterranean.
The Chefs of ZuZu are inspired by fresh, seasonal
ingredients and places an emphasis on using organic
and sustainable produce, seafood and meats.

<u>YOUNTVILLE</u>

A little over 50 miles north of San Francisco. Less
than 3,000 people call this place "home." You
wouldn't think so in the summer, which is why it's a

great place to visit off-season. Great deals not only in the restaurants, but in area lodgings as well. There are 6 Michelin stars in little Yountville, and they are all within a few blocks of each other.

AD HOC
6476 Washington St., Yountville: 707-944-2487
www.thomaskeller.com/ad-hoc
CUISINE: American
DRINKS: Full bar
SERVING: Dinner, Sunday brunch
One of premier Chef **Thomas Keller's** establishments, this one is quite informal, down to the point that there's only one brief, 4-course menu each night. But worry not, the same exacting standards regarding ingredients are employed here as in his other, more formal, eateries. The menu changes nightly, features family-style cuisine, If you're lucky, the night you're there they'll have the chicken fricassee or the buttermilk fried chicken or the "pork 'n pickles" (baby back ribs, sweet potato mostarda with lots of pickles to cut the fat. Oh, my!
ADDENDUM is the small take-out shack behind Ad Hoc (closed in winter; opens in April) where you can pick up boxed lunches of fried chicken or their great BBQ for $16 Thursday through Saturday; closed Sunday-Wednesday; 707-944-1565.

BOTTEGA RISTORANTE
6525 Washington St., Yountville: 707-945-1050
www.botteganapavalley.com/
CUISINE: Italian
DRINKS: Full bar

SERVING: Lunch, Dinner
Owner Michael Chiarello works the room like a
Broadway star. (Get a table facing the kitchen; they
have the best view of the room.) The standout here is
the gnocchi.

BOUCHON BAKERY
6528 Washington St., Yountville: 707-944-2253
bouchonbakery.com/
CUISINE: French bakery
DRINKS: no booze
SERVING: 7 a.m. to 7 p.m.
All foodies know that this bakery is owned by the
famed **Thomas Keller**, owner of the **French
Laundry**. Come here for baked goods prepared using
the classic recipes: pastries, Viennoiserie, cookies,
macaroons. But also for breakfast, confections,
quiche (the ham quiche for breakfast is a standout),
sandwiches, salads, picnic baskets, even treats for
your pets.

CICCIO

6770 Washington St, Yountville, 707-945-1000
www.ciccionapavalley.com
CUISINE: Pizza / Italian
DRINKS: Full Bar
SERVING: Dinner nightly, closed Mon & Tues
PRICE RANGE: $$
Specializing in wood-fired pizzas, this busy eatery
also offers a menu of Italian entrees made from
locally sourced ingredients and great vegetable
dishes.

FRENCH LAUNDRY

6640 Washington St. (at Creek St.), Yountville: 707-
944-2380
www.thomaskeller.com/tfl
CUISINE: American; French; Michelin rated

DRINKS: beer & wine

SERVING: lunch on weekends 11-1; dinner nightly from 5:30; DRESS CODE: don't even think about jeans or shorts or slovenly dress; men ought to bring a jacket, even a tie if you want to fit in. Jackets are even required at lunch.

Get ready for the meal of your life. All professional foodies know about this very expensive Thomas Keller eatery located in a wonderful setting in the wine country. Reserve as far ahead as you can, because it's murder to get in. But once you do, you'll be treated to one of the best dining experiences of your life. You do tend to get the feeling you're in church when you're here, so reverent are the diners and so focused are the staff. But just surrender to Keller's prix-fixe menu of 9 courses. You'll be amused at the tiny portions (you don't exactly need a microscope to see them), but they all add up to a very filling meal by the time you finish. And, much more important, an experience you'll *never* forget. When Keller dies, people will weep. $325 per person, when we went to press, service included (but not wine, let me hasten to add).

OTTIMO
6525 Washington St, Yountville, 707-944-0102
www.ottimo-nv.com
CUISINE: Italian/Pizza
DRINKS: Beer & Wine
SERVING: Lunch, Early Dinner (11a.m – 5 p.m.)
PRICE RANGE: $$
Michael Chiarello's Italian eatery & market offers a unique dining experience. The market offers a variety

of wares and food from kiosks set up around the
dining area. Select from pizza, salads, mozzarella,
salumi, and espresso drinks. Creative pizza choices
like the "sloppy Joe-seppe" pizza served with spicy
Calabrian sausage.

REDD WOOD
6755 Washington St., Yountville: 707-299-5030
www.redd-wood.com
CUISINE: Pizza, American
DRINKS: Full bar
SERVING: Lunch, Dinner
The décor looks like it's just a lot of old junk, but that
mailbox over there used to stand in front of Robert
Mondavi's house. And yes, it's pizza, but it's pizza by
a Michelin starred chef named Richard Reddington.

RUTHERFORD

LA LUNA MARKET & TAQUERIA
1153 Rutherford Rd, Rutherford, 707-963-3211
www.lalunamarket.com

CUISINE: Mexican / Convenience store
DRINKS: Beer & Wine Only
SERVING: Breakfast, Lunch, early dinner
PRICE RANGE: $
Little Mexican market and taqueria that attracts all levels of society because the food is so incredibly tasty. Here you'll see famous winemakers mixing and mingling with guys who work in the vineyards, forklift operators, local cops. Order your food to go or eat at one of the picnic tables at the back of the market. The quesadillas are the best. Nachos are huge and tasty.

ST. HELENA

ACACIA HOUSE
Las Alcobas Hotel
1915 Main St, Saint Helena, 707-963-7000
www.marriott.com
CUISINE: American (New)
DRINKS: Full Bar
SERVING: Breakfast, Lunch & Dinner
PRICE RANGE: $$
Located in the hotel housed in a century-old building dripping with rustic charm, this unique restaurant offers a creative seasonal menu. There's also room service overnight, including such items as caviar and Champagne and grilled cheese sandwiches. Favorites: Cornish hen and Risotto, but they are justifiably famous for their special preparation of duck breast. Great desserts like Peach leaf ice cream with a peach tart.

ARCHETYPE
1429 Main St, St Helena, 707-968-9200
www.archetypenapa.com
CUISINE: American (New)
DRINKS: Full Bar
SERVING: Lunch & Dinner; closed Mon & Tues
PRICE RANGE: $$
Formerly **French Blue**, this neighborhood eatery
offers an Americana menu. Most of the dishes are
prepared from the wood-burning grill or the wood-
burning oven. Menu list includes everything from
sliders to wood-charred rib eyes.

THE CHARTER OAK
1050 Charter Oak Ave, St Helena, 707-302-6996
www.thecharteroak.com
CUISINE: American (New)
DRINKS: Full Bar
SERVING: Dinner, Lunch Fri - Sun
PRICE RANGE: $$$
Family-style dining with a simple seasonal menu
including grilled meats, vegetables from the farm,
local wines and creative cocktails. Wood burning
oven is a feature here, with lots of smoked specialties.
Favorites: Chicken brined in buttermilk and grilled
slowly; Ribs smoked to perfection; and their
homemade carrot cake. NOTE: 20% Gratuity added
to all checks.

FARMSTEAD AT LONG MEADOW RANCH
738 Main St, St Helena, 707-963-4555
www.longmeadowranch.com

CUISINE: American (Traditional)
DRINKS: Full Bar
SERVING: Lunch & Dinner
PRICE RANGE: $$
Just off the town's main street is this almost perfect
farm-to-table eatery set in a renovated barn and plant
nursery with an outdoor patio (weather permitting).
The food comes from the Long Meadow Ranch's
working farm in nearby Rutherford. Favorites:
Castroville artichokes and Grass-fed steak tartare.
Nice selection of sides and wines.

GILLWOODS CAFÉ
1313 Main St., St. Helena: 707-963-1788
www.gillwoodscafe.com/
CUISINE: Breakfast & Lunch Diner

DRINKS: Beer & Wine
SERVING: Breakfast, Lunch
A local favorite serving the best breakfast in town.
Good variety of sandwiches for lunch. Prompt
service.

GOOSE AND GANDER
1245 Spring St, St Helena, 707-967-8779
www.goosegander.com
CUISINE: American (New)
DRINKS: Full Bar
SERVING: Lunch & Dinner
PRICE RANGE: $$$
This upscale gastropub offers a creative menu of
rustic American classics. This place is also known for
its craft cocktails (served in its basement bar) &
wines. The Patio is nice in good weather. Pan-roasted
chicken breast served over a bed of smoked succotash

is out of this world. The lowly and much-maligned chicken breast never tasted so good. Don't leave without trying the Duck Fat Fries.

GRILL AT MEADOWOOD
900 Meadowood Lane, St. Helena: 877-963-3646
www.meadowood.com/
CUISINE: American
DRINKS: Wine
SERVING: Breakfast, Lunch, Dinner
Not as gussied up as the more formal restaurant, the Grill overlooks the golf course and is much more casual. Weekend brunch is a must here. Daily menu with ingredients fresh from the Meadowood garden.

GOTT'S ROADSIDE TRAY GOURMET
(formerly Taylor's)
933 Main St., St. Helena: 707-963-3486
www.gotts.com/

CUISINE: Burgers, Diner
DRINKS: Beer & Wine
SERVING: Breakfast, Lunch, Dinner
Don't let the retro burger stand "fast food joint" look of this place put you off. It serves some of the finest quality food to be found around here, and locals flock to it. The ingredients are always first rate, like the burger called the Wisconsin Sourdough, with bacon, mushrooms, cheddar, BBQ sauce and mayo on a toasted roll.

PRESS
587 St. Helena Hwy., St. Helena: 707-967-0550
www.pressthelena.com/
CUISINE: Steakhouse
DRINKS: Full bar
SERVING: Dinner
While the steaks are the big draw here, get one of their rotisserie chickens and cut it up to share.
Extensive collection of wines. Impeccable service.

THE RESTAURANT AT MEADOWOOD
900 Meadowood Lane, St. Helena: 702-967-1205
www.meadowood.com
Black truffle gnocchi with parsnip Mousse and brown
butter, king salmon with beets, Pacific black cod with
white asparagus, chanterelles, bonito. There's also a
smoked chicken that's unusual. (3 stars from
Michelin.)

ROADHOUSE 29
FREEMARK ABBEY WINERY
3020 St Helena Hwy N, Saint Helena, 707-302-3777
www.twobirdsonestonenapa.com
CUISINE: Japanese / California
DRINKS: Full Bar
SERVING: Dinner, Lunch & Dinner – Sat & Sun;
closed Tues & Wed
PRICE RANGE: $$

NEIGHBORHOOD: Downtown
Located in the **Freemark Abbey Winery,** this meat-centric restaurant features "family style" dishes and a fair wine list. The meats here are smoked with local oak and the staves from old wine barrels to create a distinctive aroma you won't soon forget. The brick walls and high vaulted ceilings give the place a great look. Their wine list tilts toward wines made nearby, many with very reasonable prices (and some not reasonable at all, LOL). Favorites: Ribeye French Dip; 'The Platter' is a big draw for smoked meat lovers—you get pulled pork (8 oz), ½ rack of St. Louis style pork ribs, and superb brisket (8 oz). On the weekends they have a slow roasted Prime Rib that melts in your mouth and an excellent horseradish sauce (nice and tart) that is heads and shoulders above others I've had. Order a side of the cornbread—it's excellent.

CALISTOGA

ALL SEASONS BISTRO
1400 Lincoln Ave., Calistoga: 707-942-9111
www.allseasonsnapavalley.com
CUISINE: American
DRINKS: Beer/ Wine
SERVING: Lunch/ Dinner
Smoked baby back ribs, braised lamb shank with crispy shallots, smoked ribeye. This was among the first restaurants in the United States to receive the Wine Spectator's prestigious "Grand Award." Seasonal and regional ingredients, sustainable farming and fishing, small production, handcrafted

wines. Can't lose with this place.

EVANGELINE
1226 Washington St, Calistoga, 707-341-3131
www.evangelinenapa.com
CUISINE: Cajun/Creole/French
DRINKS: Full Bar
SERVING: Dinner; Lunch on Sat & Sun
PRICE RANGE: $$
Cozy bistro atmosphere is lots of fun and offers
indoor and outdoor dining (mostly outdoor). It's
really hard to get a table in peak season. Book well
ahead. Favorites: Duck confit and Lamb shank. Nice
wine list. Great choice for weekend brunch.
Reservations recommended.

**LAKEHOUSE RESTAURANT AT CALISTOGA
RANCH**
580 Lommel Road, Calistoga, 855-942-4220
https://calistogaranch.aubergeresorts.com/dining/

CUISINE: American (New)
DRINKS: Full Bar
SERVING: Breakfast, Lunch & Dinner
PRICE RANGE: $$$$
As Calistoga Ranch's private lakeside restaurant (it overlooks Lake Lommel), guests enjoy a rare sophisticated experience in a rustic setting. Favorites: Tai Snapper and Sonoma Duck Breast. Nice wine selection.

SAM'S SOCIAL CLUB
1712 Lincoln Ave, Calistoga, 707-942-4969
www.samssocialclub.com
CUISINE: American (New)
DRINKS: Full Bar
SERVING: Breakfast, Lunch & Dinner
PRICE RANGE: $$

Upscale eatery at **Indian Springs Resort** offering a meu of New American fare. Every meal is good here. Nice cocktail selection.

SOLBAR
In **Solage Resort**
755 Silverado Tr., Calistoga: 707-226-0860
solagecalistoga.com
CUISINE: American
DRINKS: Full Bar
SERVING: Breakfast/ Lunch/Dinner
Try the Maitake mushroom pizza here. This place is your best option in these parts for great pizza, and it's the only pizza available on the Silverado Trail. The dough at Solbar is based upon a biga-style starter, which cultivates and propagates the yeasts, developing a more complex flavor within the crust. Traditionally, Italian bakers use a biga starter for making ciabatta bread, and Solbar's pizza crust definitely features some ciabatta-like characteristics.

WHERE TO SHOP

DID YOU FIND AN INTERESTING PLACE?
If you discover a place you think I should check out
on my next visit, drop me a line, will you? I'll
mention your name if I end up listing it.
andrewdelaplaine@mac.com

750 WINES
1224 Adams St Suite C, St Helena, 707-963-0750
www.750wines.com

750 Wines, named after the size of a normal wine bottle – 750 ml, this is the only wine shop in St Helena. This specialty shop is for serious wine enthusiasts and collectors. Here you'll find special labels such as Araujo, Grace Family, Lail, and Robert Foley, lots of labels from small producers you're not likely to find anywhere else. The profits are donated to the Jameson animal-rescue facility.

BACK ROOM WINES
1000 Main St., Suite 100, Napa: 877-322-2576
backroomwines.com/
Great series of wine tastings and other wine-related events. Perfect store to buy wine to take back home.

KARA'S CUPCAKES
610 1st St Suite 19, Napa, 707-258-2253
www.karascupcakes.com
There are cupcakes and then there are Kara's cupcakes. Creative cupcakes in design and flavor usually locally sourced ingredients. Try the chocolate cupcake filled with strawberries and cream. Cupcakes come in regular or mini sizes, flavors include: banana caramel, carrot cake and key lime pie flavors. Shop early as popular flavors sell out.

MA(I)SONRY
6711 Washington St., Yountville: 707-944-0889
maisonry.com/

There are only 3 stone buildings in Yountville, and this 1904 structure built as a private house or manor is one of them. Inside, you'll find a wide array of furnishings—some old, some new, and some representing some of today's top designers. They also have wine tastings ($10 and up) that include a carefully selected list, including owner Michael Polenske's **Blackbird Vineyards** wines which closely mirror Pomerol. Beautiful gardens in the back. Don't forget to go upstairs. You'll find a lot of surprises there, including costumes (oil on paper) painted by Ralph Lauren's nephew, Greg Lauren.

NAPA VALLEY COFFEE ROASTING COMPANY

1400 Oak Ave., St. Helena: 707-963-4491
948 Main St., Napa, 707-224-2233
www.napavalleycoffee.com/
The best coffee possible. Made-to-order espresso drinks and freshly brewed coffee, pastries and cookies. Custom roasts bagged to go.

OXBOW PUBLIC MARKET

610 & 644 1st St, Napa, 707-226-6529
www.oxbowpublicmarket.com
A 40,000 square foot marketplace with an outdoor deck with seating along the Napa River. Here you find a great selection of local food vendors, artisan cafes, and organic produce from local farms.

STEVE'S HARDWARE & HOUSEWARES
1370 Main St., St. Helena: 707-963-3423
www.acehardware.com
Your local Ace Hardware for all of your hardware
and household needs.

THREE TWINS ICE CREAM
610 1st St #1, Napa, 707-257-8946
www.threetwinsicecream.com
Popular local chain selling their delicious fresh
organic ice cream in a variety of tasty flavors.

WOODHOUSE CHOCOLATE
1367 Main St., St. Helena: 800-966-3468
www.woodhousechocolate.com/
Chocolates, they're special here. Luscious, delectable
handmade chocolates.

COOKING CLASSES

DID YOU FIND AN INTERESTING PLACE?
If you discover a place you think I should check out
on my next visit, drop me a line, will you? I'll
mention your name if I end up listing it.
andrewdelaplaine@mac.com

**THE CULINARY INSTITUTE OF AMERICA
AT GREYSTONE**
2555 Main St., St. Helena: 707-967-1100
www.ciachef.edu/cia-california/
One- and Two-Day Programs. Invigorating Mornings

in the Kitchen. You'll don chef's whites and head right into the kitchen for lecture, hands-on cooking, and food and wine pairings. There's no shortage of fascinating topics to explore, from the cuisines of Northern California to healthy sustainable eating and live-fire grilling.

You'll enjoy lecture, hands-on cooking, and a wine tasting and sensory analysis session, and come away with a better understanding of the flavors of California.
Tuition varies for 1 and 2-day programs.

ATTRACTIONS

DID YOU FIND AN INTERESTING PLACE?
If you discover a place you think I should check out
on my next visit, drop me a line, will you? I'll
mention your name if I end up listing it.
andrewdelaplaine@mac.com

ART WALK
www.townofyountville.com
This is a collection of three dozen sculptures that run
up and down the street downtown.

BEAU WINE TOURS
1754 2nd St, Ste B, Napa, 707-257-0887
beauwinetours.com

Looking for something a little more economical than your own private limo?

Interested in meeting other people and making friends on a fun Daily Tour?

Daily wine tour in the Napa Valley. Full day of wine tasting. Each tour starts with free champagne served on-board one of their cars or buses. The guide takes you to four boutique wineries. Includes a picnic lunch from the Girl & the Fig Restaurant, served at one of the many hidden-gem locations in the valley (usually among vineyard views, garden terraces or wine cellars depending on weather). Lunches are served "family style" allowing everyone to pick and choose from a variety of sandwiches, side salads, and desserts. Fees apply.

BLUE NOTE NAPA
1030 Main St, Napa, 707-880-2300
www.bluenotenapa.com
Highbrow jazz club & music venue in historic location, with a New American eatery downstairs.

CALISTOGA FARMER'S MARKET
1234 Washington St., Calistoga, 707-942-8892
www.visitnapavalley.com/event/calistoga-farmers-market/2277/
Saturdays, 8:30 a.m. - 12 Noon; May 7 through October 29. Sharpsteen Plaza located across from the City Hall in downtown Calistoga.

CASTELLO DI AMOROSA
4045 St. Helena Hwy., Calistoga: 707-967-6272
www.castellodiamorosa.com

A crazy winemaker, **Dario Sattui,** for all his life in love with medieval architecture, built this fantastic castle of over 100 rooms (I think I remember that it has over 120,000 square feet), all in the style of the ancient castle-fortresses of Northern Italy. An $18 admission fee gives you not only a tour of the place, but also a tasting of 5 of their wines. There's a Knight's Room featuring frescoes, a torture chamber, a chapel (actually used for weddings and whatnot), extensive wine cellars—all of it will give you a feeling that you're FAR away from the Napa Valley.

CRANE PARK
360 Crane Avenue, St. Helena: 707-967-2792
www.cityofsthelena.org/parksrec/page/crane-park
They offer nightly bocce here that's popular with

locals. As Francis Ford Coppola said, "There are 138 local teams and it's really fun. We like bocce because you can play holding the ball in one hand and a glass of wine in the other." 10 acre park with 6 lighted tennis courts, 4 lighted bocce ball courts, 2 Little League baseball fields, horse shoe pits, children's play ground and individual and group picnic areas. Also site of **St. Helena Farmers Market**, open from 7:30 to 11:30 a.m. every Friday, May through October.

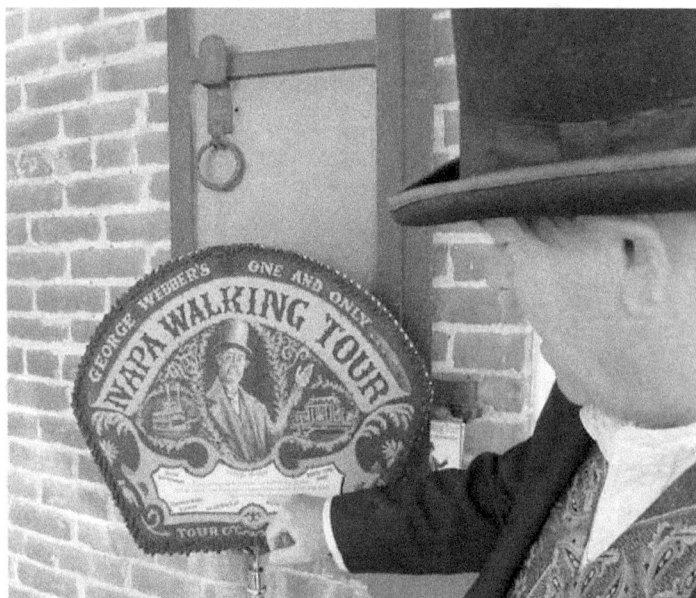

GOURMET NAPA WALKING TOUR
415-312-1119
COST: inquire for current fee
gourmetwalks.com
There is more to Napa than just wine tasting.
Welcome to the FIRST culinary walking tour in Wine

Country, for those who know that California cuisine is just as sought after as its wine. Tour covers downtown Napa. Get the fascinating history of this riverfront town, one where celebrity chefs intermingle with organic farmers and boutique winemakers. You start at the **Oxbow Market**, where there's a seasonal bounty of California specialty foods and produce. Tour crosses the Napa River to visit 19th century historic buildings that weathered Prohibition to showcase the latest trends in California food and wine. You'll leave the tour with a carefully curated list of Wine Country restaurant recommendations and recipes for your next meal. NOTE: Customers must be over 21 and bring valid ID to participate in wine tastings.

NAPA DOWNTOWN FARMERS' MARKET
195 Gasser Dr., Napa: 707-501-3087
www.napafarmersmarket.org
The Napa Certified Farmers Market has been bringing fresh, local produce, specialty foods and artisan crafts to the City of Napa, California, for more than 20 years. Tuesdays and Saturdays from 7:30 a.m. until noon

NAPA VALLEY BALLOONS

One California Drive, Yountville: 707-944-0228
COST: inquire for current fee
napavalleyballoons.com
Voted "Best Balloon Ride" 1996-2010. Featured on the Today Show, Oprah and the Travel Channel. The company trusted to fly Chelsea Clinton. Pre-flight & post-flight breakfast and champagne. Comfortable state-of-the-art aircraft. They've been flying hot air balloons over the Napa Valley for about 30 years. They have FAA certified pilots and aircraft, a professional staff and an impeccable safety.

NAPA VALLEY BIKE TOURS

6500 Washington St., Bldg. B, Yountville: 707-251-8687

COST: Fees vary

napavalleybiketours.com

Full-service bike tour company since 1987. They offer single-day guided winery tours by bike, self-guided winery tours by bike and bike rentals, as well as custom Napa Valley vacation packages.

NAPA VALLEY OPERA HOUSE

1030 Main St., Napa: 707-880-2300

nvoh.org

Napa Valley Opera House is the jewel of the Valley that showcases excellence in music and performing arts for audiences of all ages including world-class musical theatre, plays, chamber music, jazz, opera, dance and family programs. In a place where the nightlife is, shall we say, limited, you'd do well to see what's playing when you're in the area.

NAPA VALLEY WINE TRAIN
1275 McKinstry St., Napa: 707-253-2111
COST: Varies upon lunch/ dinner and car chosen to ride in
winetrain.com

The tracks upon which the Napa Valley Wine Train runs were originally built in the 1860s to bring guests to the hot spring resort town of Calistoga. While the track to Calistoga no longer exists, much of the rest of the route is unchanged. Due to the immense influence that rail transport had over the development of the communities and wineries of the Napa Valley, there is no shortage of sights to see during the 3-hour journey to St. Helena. Five towns; Napa, Yountville, Oakville, Rutherford, and St. Helena; and numerous wineries can be seen through the large picture windows on board the Wine Train.

 VISTA DOME - Intimate, special and above the

crowd. Almost 180-degree Napa Valley vistas under the antique dome windows. Enjoy wine pairing events and romantic moonlight dinners.

GOURMET EXPRESS - Relive the luxury and tradition of railroad dining as the steward seats you in the Gourmet car. White linen service for half your journey. The other? The comfort of the lounge car.

SILVERADO - Taste the barbeque side of Napa Valley gourmet in the Silverado car. This open-air railcar has a relaxed atmosphere, with a western theme and sliding windows.

Take the Ferry from San Francisco. Getting here from San Francisco could not be easier - or more pleasant. Hop on a ferry and enjoy a Bay cruise on your way to the Wine Train.

You must make reservations at least a day in advance.

The San Francisco-Napa Connection is available only with their lunch trains. Reservations required. Leave San Francisco at 8:30, be back by 7. Depending on the time of year, you might take the Ferry or the Bus. Check the "Mode of Transportation Table" for details. Both the Ferry and the Bus will drop you off in Vallejo where you will board the Napa Valley Wine Train Shuttle.

SAFARI WEST
3115 Porter Creek Rd., Santa Rosa: 707-579-2551
COST: Varies by season.
safariwest.com
Here in the heart of California's wine country... in the field of wheat-colored grass, on the slopes of rolling green hills, among the trees and ranches and

vineyards is where you will find the essence and spirit of Africa. Not a zoo...not a drive through park...this is the home of Nancy and Peter Lang. A captivating tapestry of raw sounds and earthy smells; a magic place with the sights and sounds of the Serengeti where the air is filled with melodious chirps from the aviary, squawking calls from gregarious parrots, and a occasional lemur screech. An African style oasis where guests experience a rare sense of freedom and gain renewed inspiration. Enjoy all the creature comforts when you spend the night in one of their luxury tents—"It's like having a tent over your room." Pale-green canvas walls enclose plush beds, hot showers and rustic but elegant trappings. There are polished wood floors, custom wood-slab countertops in the private bathrooms and one-of-a kind hand hewn furniture. There is nothing more magical than falling asleep to the sounds of a kookaburra and waking to the resounding love-songs of the sarus cranes. Removed from televisions, computer screens and even cell-phone reception, gazing over the rolling hills and roaming herds from your private tent deck is the ultimate in high-definition viewing.

SILO'S MUSIC ROOM
530 Main St., Napa: 707-251-5833
COST: Cover charges depends on entertainment
silosnapa.com
Premier Music Room and Wine Bar features the best in live Rock, Motown, Reggae, and Jazz alongside Napa's finest wines and draft beers. Conveniently located right in Downtown Napa at the Historic Napa

Mill and Napa River Inn. Open Wednesday through
Saturdays.

ST. HELENA'S FARMERS' MARKET
Crane Park St., Helena: 707-486-2662
sthelenafarmersmkt.org
Fridays, 7:30 a.m. till Noon; May through October.
Rain or Shine. Located in Crane Park, just south of
town behind the St. Helena High School.

V MARKETPLACE
6525 Washington St, Yountville, 707-944-2451
www.vmarketplace.com
Napa Valley's most beautiful specialty retail complex
surrounded by lush picnic gardens, gorgeous water
features and lovely meandering cobblestone
walkways, all in an enclosed environment. The
complex includes a variety of specialty shops, four
galleries, three restaurants, and two wine tasting bars.
Shops include: Kollar's Chocolates, A Little
Romance, and Authentic Panama Hats and Fedoras.

WINE COUNTRY BUS TOURS
415-440-8687
COST: varies by age.
www.city-sightseeing.us/categories/wine-country-tours
Napa and Sonoma are world famous for their fine wine and beautiful scenery. Learn about wine from their expert guides as you travel north to the wine country. You'll learn the history of winemaking, from the early Spanish missionaries who brought grape vines from Europe to the Forty-Niners who served wines in their saloons. You will tour wineries and see how grapes are picked, crushed, blended and bottled. You'll walk through beautiful vineyards with your tour guide and then taste the finished product – wine-tasting fees included. There will be time for lunch at Historical Sonoma Square or Vintage 1870 in the heart of Napa. ALL TOURS include pick-up and drop-off at most San Francisco Hotels. Approx. 9 hours. Departs: 9 a.m.

WINERIES

There are over 300 wineries in the region, but I'm not
going to give you anything like a comprehensive list.
Here are the ones I'd choose from if I had a limited
amount of time to spend in the Valley.

BEAULIEU VINEYARD
1960 Saint Helena Hwy, Rutherford, 707-257-5749
www.bvwines.com

Established by Georges de Latour and his wife in 1900, this vineyard offers some of the finest California wines, particularly their Rutherford Cabernet Sauvignon. You can visit the oldest building on the property that dates back to 1885. There's also the **Heritage Room**, which lays out the history of the wine industry in the Napa Valley. Treat yourself to the VIP Wine tasting for the best experience. Fee waived for Wine Club Members.

BLACK STALLION
4089 Silverado Trl, Napa, 707-227-3250
www.blackstallionwinery.com
Located on a historic equestrian estate, this small-batch winery offers a circular tasting bar and a terrace. The winery features both white and red wines as well as Rosé and Muscat. There's a demonstration vineyard that allows you to analyze leaf shape and cluster size and examine over a dozen different varietals. If you top for a snack, get one of the tasty

flatbreads. Great stop during warmer months. Gift shop onsite.

BUEHLER VINEYARDS
820 Greenfield Rd, Saint Helena, 707-963-2155
www.buehlervineyards.com
Allow approximately 2-3 hours for your experience here – great tour and tasting. No charge for tour/tasting but you'll probably end up buying some wine at the end. Tastings & tours by appointment only. You'll find excellent values here when you buy wine.

CADE ESTATE
360 Howell Mountain Rd S, Angwin, 707-965-2746
www.cadewinery.com
Set against the backdrop of staggering Napa Valley vistas, this winery offers 5 wines – strong on cabs but the Sauvignon blanc is also good quality. It's the views from this place that will make you wish you'd

moved here years ago when real estate prices were cheap. Tasting room is open by appointment only. Moderate fee for tour and tasting – independent of wine purchase. Tasting lounge, outdoor courtyard patio that they call a living room, winery terrace and custom-built cave.

CHAPPELLET
1581 Sage Canyon Rd, Saint Helena, 707-286-4219
www.chappellet.com
Known for their excellent cab, this has a beautiful setting high up on Pritchard Hill. The winery offers a 90-minute tour/tasting. They do a seated tasting of their new releases. Curated tours offered at a variety of prices. Tours available by reservation only.

CLIFF LEDE
1473 Yountville Cross Rd, Yountville, 707=944-8642
www.cliffledevineyards.com
Known for their Poetry Cabernet Sauvignon, they also produce Sauvignon Blanc and Cabernet Sauvignon. Several experiences are offered here: Tasting bar (open daily), Veranda Table Tasting (reservations required), Backstage Tasting Lounge (more expensive/reservations required), and Front Row (Members Only). The FEL Pinot Garden is also open daily where wine is available by the glass (reservations suggested). The winery is decorated with several famous guitars and famous musician paintings.

CORISON
987 St Helena Hwy, St Helena, 707-963-0826
www.corison.com
Known for their Cabernet. Small, family-owned working winery. Open daily by appointment. Moderate price for guided tour with Library Cabernet tasting. Featured tasting flight changes frequently and highlights wines specifically chosen from their Library. The owner frequently leads the tasting sessions himself.

DARIOUSH
4240 Silverado Trail, Napa: 707-257-2345
www.darioush.com/
Darioush Khaledi, a passionate wine man, started this place in 1997 and even in that short time he has built

an exceptional winery. He grew up in the Shiraz region of Iran, and left after the revolution.

DOMAINE CHANDON
1 California Dr., Yountville: 888-242-6366
www.chandon.com
An excellent spot to stop for a tasting and to experience the first-class job they do here. The Möet et Chandon people launched this winery in 1973 to produce American sparkling wine at affordable prices and in the same manner they make it in France, what's called "methode champenoise." You'll love the gardens and art. It also has an excellent restaurant, **Etoile**, where they design the food to complement the sparklers produced here.

ETUDE
1250 Cuttings Wharf Rd, Carneros, 707-257-5782
www.etudewines.com
Known for its almost 4 decade-old legacy of high quality Pinot Noirs. Wine tasting/tours available at a variety of levels. Reservations required.

FAILIA
3530 Silverado Trail N, St Helena, 707-963-0530
www.faillawines.com
Several tasting experiences available (prices vary) in the Tasting Room, Tasting Lodge, Cave Tour (it covers 15,000 square feet) or Spotlight Tour. Spotlight Tour is the most exclusive tasting. Available by Appointment only.

FRANK FAMILY VINEYARDS

1091 Larkmead Lane, Calistoga: 707-942-0859
www.frankfamilyvineyards.com/
Their wines are really popular all over L.A. because
Rich Frank's sons Paul and Darryl are how biz execs
(Paul is executive producer of *Royal Pains*, and
Darryl is prexy of DreamWorks TV). Frank himself
was formerly president of Walt Disney Studios, so
you can see why Hollywood types flock here. Has a
wine club with over 2,000 members. While they're
noted for their high-priced Cabs, the Frank family
Napa Valley Cabernet Sauvignon sells for under $50.

HALL RUTHERFORD

56 Auberge Rd., Rutherford: 707-967-2626
COST: inquire for current fee
hallwines.com/hall-rutherford

Hall Rutherford is Craig and Kathryn Hall's stunning winery amid the legendary Sacrashe vineyard. Completed in March of 2005, this high-tech facility has been carefully designed for the production of small-lot red wine. Custom made three-to-six-ton fermenters afford their winemakers great flexibility and precision handling of vineyard blocks and the ability to micro-manage every aspect of the winemaking process. Unlike the Halls' St. Helena property, which is able to handle more significant quantities of grapes during harvest, this compact gravity-flow winery is dedicated solely to the production of rare and single vineyard red wines. The winery's 14,000 square feet of caves were designed and built by Friedrich Gruber of Gutenstein, Austria.

The caves are finished with handmade Austrian brick recovered from sites in and around Vienna. The caves showcase select works from the Halls' art collection. Deep inside the caves is a reception area for private tastings and entertaining. The room's chandelier, designed by Donald Lipski and Jonquil LeMaster, is dressed in hundreds of Swarovski crystals.

HALL WINES
401 St. Helena Hwy., St. Helena: 707-967-2626
www.hallwines.com/
Founded in 1885, noted for its classic Bordeaux varietals. Daily tours & tastings.
tour and barrel tasting offers a first hand look into the life of a wine, from barrel to bottle.

HDV
588 Trancas St, Napa, 707-251-9121
www.hdvwines.com
HdV is a venture of the Hyde Family of Napa Valley and the de Villaine Family of Burgundy. They use Burgundian winemaking techniques here. Wine tastings by appointment only.

HEITZ CELLAR
436 St Helena Hwy, St Helena, 707-963-2047
www.heitzcellar.com
This winery, famous for it consistently superior wines, practices sustainable and certified organic farming and offers a free tasting (a rarity in Napa). Nice selection of wines.

INGLENOOK WINERY

1991 St. Helena Hwy., Rutherford: 707-968-1100
www.inglenook.com/
A lot of people don't know this, but famed
"Godfather" director Francis Ford Coppola, in
addition to his eponymous winery in the Sonoma
Valley, also owns this fabled winery. It sits on 1,600
acres of prime Napa Valley vineyard land. It's been

producing highly valued cabs since the 1940s. The
filmmaker bought this winery in 2011 after it had
fallen into disrepute as a maker of cheap wines. He
now lives in a house at this winery and his plans call
for Inglenook to regain its former cachet.

JOSEPH PHELPS VINEYARDS

200 Taplin Rd., St. Helena: 707-963-2745
www.josephphelps.com
Phelps was in the construction business back in the
'60s when he first came here (to build a winery,

actually). Like a lot of other people, he fell in love with the Valley, but he did something more than dream about it. He bought some vineyards and went into a new career. This is not a place where you will see busloads of bedraggled tourists pouring into a tasting room. Here you'll need an appointment. They have several different tastings available. A beautiful winery, famous for its reds.

KENZO ESTATE
3200 Monticello Rd., Napa: 707-254-7572
www.kenzoestate.com/
Kenzo Tsujimoto bought 3,800 acres here in 1990 and had sedulously worked to put together a team that makes wines served in some of the best spots in the U.S. The first vintage, 2005, was all sent back to Japan. All the great Bordeaux varietals are represented (and some Sauvignon Blanc.)

LONG MEADOW RANCH
738 Main St, St. Helena, 707-963-4555
http://www.longmeadowranch.com/
Tour the ranch, stop by the general store, and dine at the café or Chef's Table (restaurant).
Wine tour (2 – 3-hour experience – moderate fee) – Reservations required. The food here is really good. You can even taste some of the olive oils they produce. Here you can even see live music (for a fee).

LOUIS M. MARTINI
254 St Helena Hwy, St Helena, 707-968-3362
www.louismartini.com

Home to world-class Cabernet Sauvignon, this historic winery is known as one of the first to open in the Valley after Prohibition. Tours/tastings available at a variety of prices. Reservations necessary.

NEWTON VINEYARD
2555 Madrona Ave, Saint Helena, 707-204-7423
www.newtonvineyard.com
Founded in 1977, this wine estate is located just outside of St. Helena atop Spring Mountain. The vineyard offers panoramic views of Napa Valley and beautiful English style gardens impeccably maintained. Tours and tastings are available by appointment only, but well worth it because of the stunning views you get from here you won't get anywhere else, especially Pino Solo (a single pine tree at the top of the mountain)

ORIN SWIFT CELLARS
1325 Main St, St. Helena, 707-967-9179
www.orinswift.com
Popular stop on the Napa Valley circuit with a tasting room in downtown St. Helena. Excellent selection of wines makes up for the no-frills décor, though they expertly crafted the tasting room from reclaimed materials like old pickle barrels and bleacher seats. Very knowledgeable staff.

O'SHAUGHNESSY ESTATE WINERY
Angwin, 707-965-2898
www.oshaughnessywinery.com
A beautiful state-of-the-art boutique vineyard tucked away on Howell Mountain offering visits by

appointment only. Brief tour of the 11,000-square-foot caves cut into Howell Mountain and glass-and-stone cellar before ending at the tasting lounge. Recommended stop for cab lovers.

PINE RIDGE VINEYARDS
5901 Silverado Trl, Napa, 707-252-9777
www.pineridgevineyards.com
Started in 1978 by Gary and Nancy Andrus to grow and produce Cabernet Sauvignon and other Bordeaux-style wines. Daily tours and wine tastings – reservations recommended. On Sundays the chef offers a special food and wine pairing seminar. (Like walnut-cranberry bread with duck rillete or lamb merguez on gougeres.)

QUINTESSA
1601 Silverado Trl S, Rutherford, 707-286-2730
www.quintessa.com
A beautiful family-owned wine estate located in Rutherford. It's built into the hillside, so you barely notice the place from the road. A variety of tours and tastings (prices vary) available by appointment only. Amazing wines. They only release one Bordeaux style wine a year, but the tastings include multiple years and cheeses.

RAVENA
2930 St. Helena Hwy., St. Helena: 707-967-8814
www.revanawine.com/
Cabernet Sauvignon is the name of the game here.
You have to get an appointment, but well worth the
trouble. Small, family owned producer of world-class
wines.

ROBERT MONDAVI WINERY
7801 St. Helena Hwy., Oakville: 888-766-6328
www.robertmondaviwinery.com/
Located in the heart of Napa Valley, the Robert
Mondavi Winery is part of the To Kalon vineyard.
The First Growth Vineyard produces some of the
most notable and award-winning Cabernet and Fume
Blanc wines in the world. Mondavi was one of the
first wineries to offer tours, tastings, culinary and art
programs.

RAYMOND VINEYARDS
849 Zinfandel Lane, St. Helena: 707-963-3141
http://www.raymondvineyards.com
While other wineries have their "tasting rooms," the
folks here at Raymond have gone all out to create a
dizzying array of feel-good places for you to
experience their wines. They have the Crystal Room,
the Barrel Room, the Library, the Theatre of Nature,
the Rutherford Room and the Corridor of Senses. In
the Crystal Room, for example, they have a collection
of old decanters you have to see. A crystal chandelier
(by Baccarat) hangs above you. You're flanked by
stainless steel walls and a mirrored bar. In the Red
Room club (membership is $500 for a year, and you
can bring up to 3 guests), you can slip into a private
lounge where you can play billiards, drink wine, use a
vintage pinball machine and enjoy the plushness of

more red velvet than you ever thought you'd see.

ROBERT CRAIG WINERY TASTING SALON
625 Imperial Way, Napa, 707-252-2250
www.robertcraigwine.com/tastingsalon
Intimate, low-key experience in a non-hurried
environment. Tasting salon located in downtown
Napa right on the river offering samples of Robert
Craig's silky-smooth mountain Cabernets. Open daily
by appointment. They also have the "Howell
Mountain Experience," which takes you up to a 9.5
acre vineyard above the cloud-line to 2,300 feet.

ROBERT MONDAVI WINERY
7801 Saint Helena Hwy, Oakville, 888-766-6328
www.robertmondavi.com
One of the first wineries to offer tours, tastings,
culinary and art programs with three different wine
tasting experiences. The shop is filled with wines,
olive oils, chocolates, serving platters, hats, and a
variety of gifts. Such a place of history. I enjoyed a
few very special dinners here.

ROBERT SINSKEY WINERY
6320 Silverado Trl, Napa, 707-944-9090
www.robertsinskey.com
An organic winery known for its reds. Tours and
tasting room where wines are paired with food. First
they give you a glass of wine and you take that along
as they walk you through the garden. For a more
elegant experience visit the caves for a relaxing sit-
down menu.

ROUND POND ESTATE
875 Rutherford Rd, Rutherford, 707-302-2575
www.roundpond.com
Beautiful family winery and hospitality facility
featuring dining room, tours, vineyards, gardens,
olive groves and orchards. Second story tasting
lounge offers a covered terrace with panoramic views
of the vineyards and the Mayacamas Mountains.
Great wine tastings with small bites.

SCHRAMSBERG VINEYARDS
1400 Schramsberg Rd, Calistoga, 707-942-4558
www.schramsberg.com
Beautiful manicured estate offers tours and tastings
by appointment only. Tour includes the rich history of
Schramsberg and its 120-year-old caves. Known for
its sparkling wines. Part of the experience here is an
explanation of the French process of making
Champagne, the "methode traditionelle."

SHAFER VINEYARDS
6154 Silverado Trail, Napa, 707-944-2877
www.shafervineyards.com
Tours (limited to 10 people or less) are by
reservation. Tour features a seated tasting in a room
overlooking the winery. Superb red and white wines.

SPOTTSWOODE WINERY
1902 Madrona Ave, St. Helena, 707-963-0134
www.spottswoode.com
Winery located on an historic winegrowing estate on
the western edge of St. Helena. An organically-

farmed vineyard is known for its Cabernet Sauvignon and the Spottswoode Cabernet Sauvignon. Tours of the beautiful estate (with its pre-Prohibition stone cellar) and tastings available.

STAG'S LEAP WINE CELLARS
5766 Silverado Trl, Napa, 707-261-6410
www.cask23.com
Considered a Napa Valley first-growth estate known for their estate-grown Cabernet Sauvignons. Since 1971. Buy a case and your tasting fee will be waived. Staff very knowledgeable.

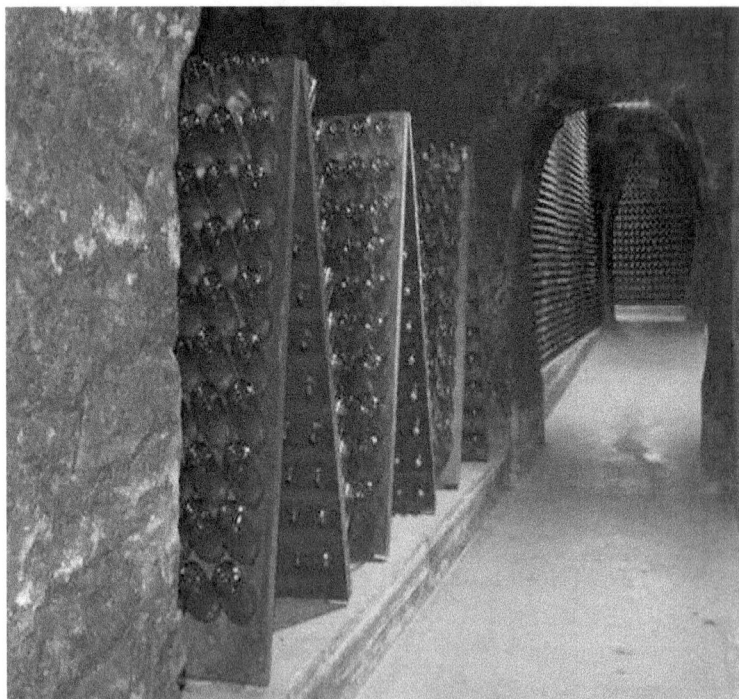

Producers of elegant vintage Pinot Noir and Chardonnay based sparkling wines in the traditional méthode champenoise. Tastings by appointment only. Tours (booked in advance) are 5 times a day. You've got to see their century old cellars.

SWANSON VINEYARDS
1271 Manley Lane, Rutherford: 707-754-4018
www.swansonvineyards.com/

This winery produces Merlot, Cabernet Sauvignon, Pinot Grigio and Dessert Wines from their Oakville vineyards. Two distinct tastings for wine lovers are offered (reservations required). Established in 1985 by the family known for Swanson Frozen Foods. The vineyards focus on Merlot, Cabernet Sauvignon, Pinot Grigio, and other intriguing varietals. Their tasting salon offers special selections along with American Caviar and other wine pairings. Great tasting experience. (Like the warm pistachios served with the wine.)

SPAS

CALISTOGA SPA HOT SPRINGS
1006 Washington St., Calistoga: 707-942-6269
calistogaspa.com
Facilities include separate Men's and Women's Spas,
four outdoor Mineral Water Pools, Exercise and

Aerobics rooms, and Conference Facilities seating forty.

EURO SPA & INN
1202 Pine St., Calistoga: 707-942-6829
eurospa.com
TripAdvisor Travelers' Choice Award Winner, 2010. Relaxing & intimate atmosphere, serene pool setting, neighboring vineyard views, true hospitality, downtown Calistoga location.

GOLDEN HAVEN HOT SPRINGS
1713 Lake St., Calistoga: 707-942-8000
goldenhaven.com
Calistoga Golden Haven Hot Springs Spa is nestled in the heart of California's Napa Valley wine country and makes the perfect Calistoga spa getaway. Come and experience the magic of the Calistoga hot springs water and rejuvenating spa treatments. After a day of touring Napa Valley, you can swim in

Their hot springs pool, relax on the sun deck under the California sun, and rejuvenate with our famous Calistoga spa treatments.

MOUNT VIEW HOTEL & SPA
1457 Lincoln Ave., Calistoga: 707-942-6877
mountviewhotel.com
Voted Best Boutique Resort by Bohemian 2010. Cabanas, Pool, Jacuzzi, Day Spa, Breakfast in Bed, Winery Suites, WIFI and more.

SPA SOLAGE
755 Silverado Tr., Calistoga: 707-266-7531
solagecalistoga.com/spa/
Health and wellness are at the heart of the Solage experience. Artfully designed and ecologically conscious, Spa Solage offers relaxing and invigorating services, including new twists on the renowned Calistoga mud and mineral water therapies.

INDEX

VINTNER'S COLLECTIVE TASTING ROOM, 40

WOODHOUSE CHOCOLATE, 63

W

Z

WINE COUNTRY BUS TOURS, 78

ZUZU, 40

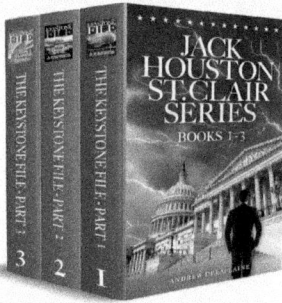

WANT 3 *FREE* THRILLERS?

Why, of course you do!

If you like these writers--
Vince Flynn, Brad Thor, Tom Clancy, James Patterson,
David Baldacci, John Grisham, Brad Meltzer, Daniel Silva,
Don DeLillo

If you like these TV series –
House of Cards, Scandal, West Wing, The Good Wife,
Madam Secretary, Designated Survivor

You'll love the **unputdownable** series about
Jack Houston St. Clair, with political intrigue, romance,
and loads of action and suspense.

Besides writing travel books, I've written political thrillers
for many years that have delighted hundreds of thousands
of readers. I want to introduce you to my work!
Send me an email and I'll send you a link where you can
download the first 3 books in my bestselling series,
absolutely FREE.

Mention **this book** when you email me.
andrewdelaplaine@mac.com